Life Stinks!

Sally McCreith

This day will never come again and anyone who fails to eat and drink and taste and smell it will never have it offered to them again in all eternity.

~ Hermann Hesse

Prologue

I've always been an animal person. I know it's a bit of a cliché, but I am that person at a party who will find the pet in the house and beeline for them. I always stroke street cats or ask strangers if I can pet their dogs. Animals tend to take to me quickly, and I derive great satisfaction from that.

The trick with most animals is a slow and gentle approach. Make them feel secure, first extend your hand, slowly. Let them have a sniff.

A sniff

One sniff from an animal can tell them all they need to know about you. Whether you will be green lit to provide and receive their affection and trust.
Isn't that remarkable, that something so coveted as the trust of another living creature could rely on smell alone?

Something you don't have much influence over when it comes to animals. Animals are not testing to see if they like your perfume or the brand of hand wash you've purchased. It's a deeper scent, one you can't control.

Before everything that happened to me, I had never truly considered the importance of smell. Not just with animals and their willingness to be petted, but in life; how much influence smell has on so many aspects of your life.

If you had asked me about a fear of losing a sense, then sight or hearing would spring to mind. I'm not here to dispute that would not be a terrible thing, it undeniably would be. I still fear it. But I fear the loss of smell too now.

No. Fear isn't the right word because this isn't a book about fear. It's about coping and overcoming. I guess appreciation for the senses, and how lucky we are to be able to see and hear. To touch, taste, smell, and experience everything in its fullest possible sense. Believe me, it is worth valuing.

I understand now, more than ever, that smell is appetite and craving. To smell is confidence, and it is comfort. It is memory and sentiment, innovative and evocative.

It is so important and should not be taken for granted, it is so precious.

I would like to dedicate this book to the people in my life who stood by me, were understanding and supportive, and always prepared to help. My journey was a difficult one, but if not for those people, it would have been so much harder.

From all this experience, I have learned to appreciate the importance of smell, but even more so to appreciate the people I love. Not that the latter was ever in doubt.

During a time when I could not sustain myself, barely able to eat, at a time when I felt my lowest; my husband and friends; you were, are, and will ever continue to be my soul food.

Chapter 1

A Pandemic in Our Lifetime

Did you ever think you would live in a time of pandemic?

I remember history lessons in school, learning about the black plague and the Spanish flu. Not really taking it seriously, feeling almost comforted that in the hundreds of years since these events, healthcare and technology had come such a long way; that any modern-day viral outbreak would be so easily containable and treatable compared to back then. It would have a very minimal impact on me or those around me.

Fast forward to March 2020. We knew things were happening, footage and media from Wuhan, China initially, but soon after reports of it spread. Italy was the next hardest hit, much closer to home.

In March 2020, I was on a countdown to my thirtieth birthday in early April. My husband, J, was taking me on a surprise Europe trip he had been planning for some time, but some miracle it was still a surprise at this point. Not Italy, he assured, as we followed the news about the spread, the various countries implementing lockdown procedures. I watched nervously as airlines started to announce travel cancellations.

Sure enough, he called a few days later to let me know the holiday was off. A few days after that, our own country went into lockdown.

I work for the National Health Service (NHS), and so was able to retain some element of normality throughout the period. Driving to work, albeit on empty roads, seeing my colleagues every day. Not that work itself was normal.

It sounds dramatic but there were days when it felt like being in the army, gearing up for war, redeployment to the 'front lines'. I can remember a briefing by medical colleagues told us there was a very real possibility that some colleagues would not make it through the other side of this, and they were right. Some were lost to covid. But we all threw ourselves in, the NHS staff were there ready to fight. Annual leave cancelled, working relentlessly late into the evenings, over weekends.

While many were furloughed enjoying the heatwave spring brought from their back gardens, we were in up to 7 days a week. Exhausted but hopeful we could see it over soon.

Those frantic workdays were broken up only by obscure weekends, visiting family at the front door, or the elation of seeing a familiar face while queuing to do your weekly shop.

The craving for social interaction grew, the desperation to connect with people manifesting in Saturday night zoom quizzes. These escalated from a casual quiz to karaoke in fancy dress. It wasn't the same, but we made the best of it. We missed one another, but technology granted us some opportunities to socialise.

Restrictions started to lift and by August there was almost a sense of normal again. A sense of hope that our lives were back, and ordinary routines could resume. For a little while there, they did, some semblance of them at least.

The first week of September, J mentioned he was feeling a bit "under the weather". Not a persistent cough or a temperature that we knew to look out for, just not quite right. We chalked it up to a heavy weekend, now that socialising was allowed once more, and didn't think any more of it. I went to work as normal. It was a few days later when he still didn't feel good that we registered him for a PCR test.

I firmly believed he didn't have Covid at the time. This disease I had seen patients dying from. At worst it was "man-flu". I arranged the test but then with frustration went home to isolate myself. I can remember thinking 'this negative result better come back soon so I can still go out this weekend'.
On the day of his test, he developed a cough, but I wondered if the invasive testing had triggered it. I was still in denial.

The test came back Friday. It was positive. We were instructed to quarantine from society but do our best to isolate from one another too. It's difficult when you share a home; nevertheless, we segregated ourselves as best we could. I slept on the couch. He was sick, he needed proper sleep, and so he got the bed.

Saturday morning, I woke up with a headache that felt like a prosecco hangover. The sort where your skull feels unhinged, the slightest movement makes it rattle inside of your head.

I am not a total stranger to headaches of this sort, but they normally follow a social evening. I had not had a drink the night before, so I decided to get myself tested. Other than the headache everything was okay, but still there was a good chance with our close contact and proximity I had caught covid too.

By Monday my test had come back positive. J was significantly worse now too. He had a full-blown cough, the sort that makes you wince for the person when you hear it. Raw. It was incessant.

We were still sleeping apart, but I would hear it through the night. For me I just felt very tired, my head still pounding.

Everything came in waves. At times I felt well enough to log onto work servers and scroll through emails. Then other times I would sit at the table with my head in my arms, unable to look at the screen.

Tuesday, day four for me was the start of the real illness. I can remember so clearly waking up, my whole body aching. Breathing deeply, my lungs crackled like wood on a fire.

My reflection looked like early Halloween makeup. Huge dark rivets beneath my eyes, lips pale. I felt weak, but not hungry. Hot but shivering at the same time. Bones like lead weights, especially my thighs. They would burn in protest when I tried to walk.

I had to climb the stairs on all fours, I had to stop about halfway up and catch my breath. Burning bones severely restricted mobility. Bottle of water and a satsuma in hand to toss into the bedroom to J. We lived off satsumas then. Praying the vitamin C would help fight it off but still light enough when you didn't have an appetite.

For as bad as I was, J was worse. Like me, he had the aches, the pains, and the feverishness. But his cough was aggressive. Somehow dry and barking, yet at the same time almost damp. It was as though you could hear the moisture in his lungs.

Those few days, I can tell you I was genuinely afraid. On more than one occasion I considered calling an ambulance. I knew how quickly it could escalate even in healthy young people. It was bad enough already and if it got any worse, we would need medical intervention. We ended up calling 111 instead and they were able to arrange antibiotics for a respiratory infection.

It was day six of Covid, where this story truly begins. On day six, my smell was gone. I was eating a satsuma and realised it had no real taste to it. Then came the recognition that I couldn't smell it either. I had heard about this being a symptom and was not overly fazed. The more pressing concern being aching bones, lungs like popping candy, and J's worsening condition.

The next few days passed by with regular rest and just trying to recoup our strength and overcome the crippling fatigue. One day I slept solidly for almost sixteen hours. We both started to see some improvement and gain more functionality after rest.

His smell and taste returned by the time were at the end of our fourteen-day isolation period. Mine, however, had not.

Chapter 2

Loss of Sense, Loss of Self

Anosmia is the complete loss of smell. There is simply nothing when you try to inhale a scent, a total absence of anything. In the early days, I would put my nose to things I knew should smell a certain way and just really inhale but I had no success.

The worst consequence of this was food carried no taste. I was aware of the foods I was eating but it was without flavour. Everything bland. I struggled to eat things that were heavy because it just felt like endless chewing. I tried to make mealtimes exciting by varying textures to substitute the lack of flavour.

At the time I was really upset. I have always loved good food, eating rich meals of diverse tastes. But food without flavour is just fuel. I would try and alternate textures because that was the only variety that was on offer to me. As such, salads tended to be the most interesting food to eat. Things like bread were ruined, if you had to chew it a lot it felt like a chore, just trudging through instead of experiencing essence.

Turning to the internet for help, there were a few suggestions on there.

Spicy food to ignite taste, this was an odd one. I have never been good with spicy food before this all happened to me. I don't have a huge spice tolerance and stay firmly in the mild section, 'one chilli' logo is my limit.

J is the opposite and opts for the hottest possible meals. If I do attempt to try them, they render me with burning ears and streaming sinuses, spluttering red-faced while he barely registers a tingle. I've always disliked being limited by my lack of heat resilience so thought maybe this would be an exciting new opportunity to be bolder with spices.

We tried a hot curry. The impact? The curry had no flavour, no taste. But I could still feel the burning. Every other part of my body reacted as I was used to at the hands of this curry. It wasn't pleasant for me. It also did not have the desired effect of reawakening my sense of smell or taste.

Burnt meals were inevitable without careful and constant observation to know I wasn't overcooking. I had no way of telling if food was safe to eat either. You don't appreciate just how reliant you become on smell to act as a sentinel, stopping you from consuming foods that might be past their best and with loss of taste too, you don't find out until it's too late.

There were some small perks to losing my sense of smell. Cleaning out the cat litter was an easier job; public bathrooms were never a risk to enter.

Yet I would have happily welcomed those smells again; if it meant being able to breathe in the scents of the kitchen and feel a rumble of anticipation in my stomach with an appetite to eat once more, to feel clean after a shower, sweet-smelling and confident. Losing that awareness of my own bodily function and hygiene left me so paranoid.

One potentially dangerous side effect was alcohol. I couldn't taste the alcohol but still experienced the buzz. If I had been so inclined, I could have chugged vodka like it was water. Not being able to taste is bizarre and disconcerting. At the time, I thought it was the worst possible thing. But that came later.

Two months after having covid and dealing with my anosmia, I was making lunch one day, mushroom soup. I remember pottering around the kitchen as the soup was warming in the microwave when suddenly a smell hit me.

The fleeting delight at the very sensation of being able to smell again was quickly replaced by disgust. This smell was awful. Like hot, rotting meat mixed with chemicals. I investigated- was it cat's litterbox?

Had something crawled into one of the cupboards and died? But no, there was nothing obvious. Then I took my soup out of the microwave and the smell got stronger. But it couldn't be the soup? Perhaps if it were chicken soup, if the chicken had gone off, I might expect a smell like this. But mushrooms? I tentatively took a mouthful and a rancid taste that mirrored the smell filled my mouth. I couldn't eat another bite.

This was my first experience of parosmia.

The smell lingered. It became constant. Stronger if there was a specific source of smell, like a freshly made meal. But always present. Relentless.

The easiest way to describe it was rotten meat laced with chemicals. Where we live, there are docks and driving through the area you are often hit with the reek of factory waste. It was very reminiscent of this only perpetually present.

Subsequently, it made food taste that way too. The more distinctive the flavour of food, the stronger the disgusting taste, and the harder it was to stomach. Every time I would put something in my mouth it just tasted off and I would feel my body heave and gag, my brain telling me to spit it out because it would make me ill. This happened with everything, both foods that could spoil, but even things like chocolate carried such a foul taste. In the early days of parosmia there was no true 'safe food'.

The coming weeks brought various dinner experiments with ranging success. My general rule became bland is best. Anything too flavoursome was off the table. Meat was the worst offender. It smelt so rotten that the very texture of meat in my mouth induced a gag reflex I could not push down. But other things too, onions, garlic. Green peppers were particularly awful.

It also extended to drinks. Red wine, once my drink of choice, was appalling. Coffee may as well have been dirt water. I was able to drink tea and water but even then, there was a lingering stale taste that eradicated enjoyment from any sustenance.

I had thought anosmia was miserable as a foodie. This was a fresh hell. It was hard not to burst into tears at dinner time. I was just forcing the starkest of foods down to maintain basic nutrition, pasta without sauce, plain bread, the blander the better.

J was so supportive. He's a wonderful cook, but I just couldn't appreciate any of his meals. He would trial foods and recipes to broaden what I could eat. He didn't get mad or fed up with me when I couldn't eat more than a few bites of food he had made, which happened often. He never felt insulted when I wretched at his dinners, he knew it was never a reflection on his cooking. I did not taste what I knew I should be. It was akin to the torment of purgatory, delicious food before me turning to rot in my mouth.

It wasn't long before I started to notice my clothes were loose. My hair thinned; my skin grew duller. My energy levels were non-existent. I was breathless all the time. The slightest things would just leave me gasping for air. I live near a beach, and we made a habit of having a nightly walk down to the beach, watching the sunset, and looping back. I often had to stop and catch my breath halfway through these gentle walks. I felt like a senile old lady rather than a 30-year-old woman.

Over time, I learned using a nasal inhaler would clear the smell slightly, and although my food tasted like menthol, it enabled me to eat slightly larger portions. Over a few months of parosmia I lost two stone. I have always had a slim frame and so it was not weight I could afford to lose, in fact I looked gaunt, my bones visibly protruded under my pale skin.

When I showered it was like rubbing my body down with juice from the butcher's shop. It was a constant mental battle reminding myself it was in my head, and that my skin and hair did not smell like that to others. That my deodorant did not smell putrid.

Nevertheless, during the contact I did have with people I felt like I kept my distance, just in case. My toothpaste tasted like ashes. Burnt and dry. I desperately wanted to have fresh breath but never got the feeling of it. I went through a lot of mints in my state of paranoia that my breath smelt to others the way it did to me, and I lived with a constant sensation of having morning breath.

In some ways at the start of parosmia, the lockdown was a blessing. Restaurants were not open for me to not be able to enjoy. We could not socialise, so avoiding contact with people was easier. But as restrictions eased, I felt my mental health decline further. I was simultaneously so happy to have some freedoms back, but it made the sting of grief for what I was missing out on that much harder.

I talked to my friends and colleagues about my experiences, and they were sympathetic of course, but it is easy to forget what others' daily experience is. Please don't get me wrong, the people in my life were amazing; husband, parents, friends.

They were my tethers that made getting up each morning worthwhile and kept me grounded in the life that I had begun to feel so disconnected from. I don't think many of them even realise how much they helped me in that time and the impact their compassion had. For that, I am eternally grateful. Should any of you be reading this, know that the love I have for you is immeasurable.

But the whole experience is difficult to truly fathom and that is why I felt the need to open up and share. To write down all the memories of a period in my life that in honesty I would much rather forget.

You don't realise how much social activity revolves around food and drink until you can't eat normally; an evening at the pub, going out for a meal, BBQs in the summer, grabbing a catch-up coffee. I found myself both longing for the normality of socialising, but also incredibly anxious about having to eat and drink. I would feel embarrassed in restaurants leaving large portions of food uneaten. I think a lot of people who didn't know me assumed I had an eating disorder. Especially given how skinny I was getting.

A surprising number of people would laugh, bemused at the condition. One thing I got sick of hearing when I mentioned the weight loss was, "Oh, I could do with having parosmia" with a jovial pull at their waistband. I know insensitivity was rarely intentional, but it was rife and made everything a harder pill to swallow. Their lack of understanding made an isolating condition even lonelier.

I got to a point where I tried to avoid talking about it. I didn't want the condition to define me. I'm not sure how successful I was at hiding it but as and when we were allowed, I started to go out. I would order the most boring thing on a menu if we went out, sneaking hits of my nasal inhaler behind a napkin. I remember being in the pub with friends wincing at my glass of wine which tasted like nail polish remover.

I would often cry in the mirror getting ready at the sight of my protruding ribs and diminished curves, and dress in layers to disguise it to others. My favourite clothes that I felt good in would just hang off me, fit me all wrong. I had to buy a few new clothes to better fit me, but I was so reluctant to do it. Spending money on this new frame almost felt like accepting it was the new me and I didn't want to. I was a shell of myself, trying to pretend everything was normal.

For the most part, when I did speak about it, I talked about the bad smell of parosmia concerning food and the impact there. I suppose it was the most significant. There was one part I didn't discuss with anyone, but I feel like it is important to mention it here. It was something you don't consider with a loss or change of smell, but it the impact was huge.

Loss of connection. I am a tactile person. Connection is huge to me; I've always been sensitive to people around me and the interaction between us. Sometimes, often, words don't cut it, sometimes squeezing someone's hand, enveloping them in a hug; it's just so much more powerful.

To some extent I was already mourning this across the course of the pandemic, seeing friends from two metres apart. Desperate to reach out and embrace them but wanting to keep them safe. Thankfully, for the course of the pandemic, the one person I still could hug and be close to was J.

But parosmia, seemingly intent on taking everything left from me, affected that too. Yes, there was the feeling that I had bad breath and smelt bad which made willingness for intimacy and closeness difficult. The lingering odour of rot is a real mood killer and there was no masking it.

That was just something I had to repeatedly deny to myself, a constant internal monologue the smell wasn't real. I could probably have managed if that was the only factor, but it wasn't.

Have you ever gone in for a kiss with someone, and there's that smell? I'm not talking about the smell of their breath or if they're wearing strong aftershave. I don't think consciously you even realise it's a smell because the impact it has is more of a feeling.

Right before you kiss someone you have feelings for, it's a sweetness that overtakes you, such an intoxicating smell. I've been with my husband for over ten years; I delight that I still get that smell and sensation every time we kiss. It's an almost giddiness, stomach flutters like butterflies. The scent of passion, affection, love.

I remember feeling very, *very* aware of the absence of that. I can say with absolutely certainty it was in no way because of a loss of love for him. The habitual memory of every stolen kiss and intimate moment across more than a decade was replaced with a foreign smell I no longer recognised.

Because of that, those periods of intimacy didn't feel the same, the familiarity and comfort of him vanished. It makes it difficult. Despite what you try and convince yourself, that lack of familiar smell in an environment so vulnerable to sensation can create involuntary tension.

It was something else I struggled to enjoy, love, because it simply didn't feel right. That was what broke my heart most of all. This invisible barrier parosmia had created for me against the thing I hold most dear above all else.

No surprise then, how after around six months of living with parosmia I was at an all-time low. It was another part of the experience that I didn't discuss too openly. An unwillingness to let people in to how it was really making me feel.

I did not want it to define me, for people around me to tire of me always moaning about the problem. It became grief. I mourned the loss of my smell and taste as if it had died. In some ways it had.

Especially when doctors weren't sure if they could help. The reality of it being lost forever, living this way forever. It was hard not to be overcome by the sensation. The pain of loss, and the anger seeing people not take covid seriously, call it a hoax when I was living a nightmare. That there were days I quite genuinely felt like I could not carry on living like this. The thought of spending the rest of my life this way brought overwhelming grief and my mind went to the darkest of places.

By this point I felt as though I was not living, merely existing, I felt almost entirely empty.

Chapter 3

Media Attention

It's something we're ingrained with I think that going off sick is a negative thing. I suppose in some ways it is. But the thought of having to call in sick has always given me genuine anxiety.

The times I have done it have been a result of hospitalisation, and never just for a bad cold.
I think this pandemic highlighted how willing as a society we were to turn up for work despite being infectious. I was off, of course, when I had Covid, and I think if isolation wasn't a thing, I would have tried to drag myself in and eventually be sent home too poorly to continue.

But by April, over 6 months after my acute case, I was functioning. I could work. Yes, I'd be gasping for breath if I had to speak for too long in meetings or walk anywhere. I felt permanently exhausted and would struggle through brain fog to think about what I wanted to say. Not ideal in a job required to present regularly. At a moment's notice, I could get a whiff of something that would make me physically throw up.

Feeling this way, living like this, also meant I felt constantly on the verge of tears. I was an absolute shell of myself. But, I could get out of bed in the morning, drive my car, and perform to a reasonable standard my job. So, for a time I remember feeling like I couldn't go off sick. I thought people at work would think me a fraud. They had seen me "functional" in work.

So, I carried on. Each day, battling through the physical and mental exhaustion of it all, simply because I was capable. Looking back, I can't believe that I put myself in that situation. Had it been anyone else in my team telling me they felt this way I would have sent them home myself immediately. But hindsight's a wonderful thing. It has changed my perspective now; I will never get myself to that point again.

I now always look at situations with viewpoint if it was someone I cared about, what advice would I give them. I'd then take that advice myself.

I had been to the GP over the parosmia, and was told the science behind it, but nothing in the way of treatment options. As a result of other things like the laboured breathing and chronic fatigue – I was referred for various tests.

An ECG picked up an irregular heartbeat and I was told to prepare myself that covid might have caused some tissue damage and they would undertake further tests to let me know the severity of the damage. A tooth simply dropped out of my mouth which the dentist explained was likely poor circulation through vascular issues. I take good care of my teeth, it was devastating.

I was instructed not to exert myself in any way, no exercise, and even told not to get pregnant because my body would not be able to manage it. The blow that this condition was starting to have on all aspects of my life became overwhelming. To some extent everyone's life was put on hold by the pandemic, but it was cutting deeper for me. I was, in some senses quite literally, falling apart.

At a further GP session, when things were becoming truly overwhelming, I was once again told they couldn't help me; I broke down sobbing and was recommended anti-depressants. This alone was heart-breaking.

I declined. To me, masking the situational depression arising from my condition was not helpful. I needed to fix whatever was wrong with me or I would be reliant on pills for the rest of my days.

I've been through my fair share of bad spells in my lifetime, periods of lowness; but I would generally describe myself as a positive person. Certainly, a resilient person. Yet I could feel that seeping away as things felt more and more hopeless.

I did eventually cave and end up taking a few weeks off sick from work over the period. I'd reached a point where any amount of walking even to the kitchen to make a drink I would feel breathless. I was also starting to experience extreme dizziness when I stood up; to the point one day I hit the deck completely, bashing my head in the process.

On a few occasions, I found myself welling up and getting tearful about my situation, which left me dreadfully embarrassed, so I went off.

One of my friends and work colleagues knew someone who was writing an article on long covid and passed my information over. It seemed a small thing, but I was happy to talk for a few minutes about what I was going through.

I think when you are young and healthy it can be a bit easy to be complacent about covid. I knew people who viewed the whole thing as 'an opportunity for two weeks off work "isolating". Awareness of some of the wider side effects they could be at risk of seemed important to get out there.

For me, this was the match I needed to start the fire. My article blew up. In the space of twenty-four hours, I was approached to be on the news, the radio and feature in the campaign.

If you know me, you will know that being interviewed on TV or radio is not my comfort zone. I am not one for being in the spotlight. I'm a people watcher, a good listener; and so better in the background observing than front and centre.

But this was an opportunity, to spread awareness to those complacent. An opportunity to prompt further research about parosmia, which could lead to a cure. An opportunity to give comfort to anyone going through the same thing, so that they might know they weren't alone. So, I agreed.

On Thursday 3rd June 2021 – I appeared on Good Morning Britain, BBCNW Lunch, and was the main feature on BBC North West Tonight, as well as an afternoon health segment with their healthcare lead. I did interviews on BBC Radio Merseyside, Radio City, and Global Radio. I appeared in the Spread the Facts advert campaign which ran adverts and posters.

It was exhausting, but so good to have a platform where I could be open. Speaking about my experience came more easily than I realised. Like turning on a tap, my experience of the past few months just flowed out of me. Some of it was hard to talk about, and I had to force myself to maintain composure. But I was never short of things to speak about; in fact, I could have said more.

That night I started to watch some of the clips, and immediately had to stop. It was a bit of a shock, to see myself. I know it's not uncommon to not like the sound of your voice being played back or seeing a photo of yourself, and it was that to some extent. But for me it was how skinny I was, how dull everything was; hair, eyes, skin, missing tooth. I couldn't recognise myself.

I saw a picture of myself on a poster encouraging vaccination and I just felt so haggard looking in them. I remember thinking do I really look that old? Hating my figure, my chest was flat and bones visible even under clothes.

While I didn't have aspirations in life to be the face of a campaign, I guess in my imagination being the face of something I would associate with a more glamorous version of myself. All scrubbed up , looking my best. Instead, here I was, scattered across media the worst version of myself. An image of myself I barely recognised.

When the media used old photos from before I got sick, the girl portrayed looked like a different, healthier, and happier person. She was a different person, someone I longed to have back.

There was something good about being able to voice the impact. A lot of people approached me to say thank you for speaking up about it. One woman messaged me, thrilled, as she had been experiencing parosmia and attended a GP who told her there were no issues with her sinuses. In essence, they implied it was all in her head.

Knowing the condition had a name provided her some much-needed sanity. That was a good feeling. As tough as a time as it was for me, I knew there was a problem. People around me knew and could try and support me. I can't imagine how disorienting it would be to experience the distortion without context.

Unfortunately, there was a lot of backlash. Let me tell you, I knew all about internet trolls before all this. But the volume, the extent, the magnitude of them, it came as a shock. I'm sad to say for every positive response, every grateful person; there was someone with something negative to say, some unwarranted attack both about the content of my discussion but personal affronts too.

To give you an idea, listed below are some of the
actual internet comments I read; before I decided to
stop reading.

Liar

Attention seeker

Irresponsible / Dangerous

"She looks like she smells of rotten meat"

"Maybe she just doesn't wash"

Secret smoker

Anorexic / Bulimic

Actress / Faker

Exaggerating

Whining baby / Melodramatic

Rotten Meat *Slut*

That last one was sort of the line in the sand of
reading what the 'general population' had to say.

I can't comprehend reading an article/watching an
interview about someone experiencing the smell of
rotten meat constantly, and totally unprovoked calling
them a 'rotten meat slut'.

In fact, the absurdity of me made me laugh, and I guess truly twigged that the people saying these things were the ones with the problem. I was telling my story. I wasn't forcing my opinions on anyone. Yet people defended theirs, aggressively so.

I did stop looking after this, but I know these types of comments came in their droves. I've always thought about victims of certain crimes in the past; why people never spoke up straight away. It always baffled me. This helped me understand. Inevitable backlash.

Even if you have done nothing wrong. You can be totally innocent. Just getting the justice you so rightly deserve. But there will be someone with something to say. You have to decide whether you are willing to accept that anyway. Does it justify the means?

For me, in spite of it all, it absolutely did. For one, it helped people. I've talked about how lonely parosmia was, and there was a comfort to be found that other people were experiencing it and understood the full magnitude beyond what you could hear or read about it.

It might have been a small handful of people but even if it just helped one then it was worth it. If it made some people stop and think or exercise more caution when it came to covid, it was worth it.

Beyond that, it proved more than worth it on a personal level.

The day after all the media madness, I got an email. An email I remember now, bursting into tears the moment I read it. Not because it was offensive or aggressive like some of the other comments. But because it said,

"I think I can help you."

Chapter 4

The Treatment

I had gone down the road of medical help already to no avail. The tests I had underwent had been largely inconclusive – telling me there were issues but giving me no solutions, no treatment, no hope.

A few people recommend alternative treatments to me after my time on the media and I agreed to absolutely all of it.

They ranged from exposure to pure oxygen to eating burnt oranges and antler scrapings. The cost didn't matter. There was no sum of money I wasn't willing to spend even if it meant getting into debt, nothing I would not do to get better. I willingly tried it all. For me, these things did not yield results.

Throughout the months of parosmia I had been no stranger to trying any solution the internet had to offer me. I had spent hundreds of pounds on supplements, CBD oils, and smell-training kits. I saw snippets of progress with some things.

We would sit in the evenings, my eyes closed, sniffing the essential oils. I would have to guess what flavour the bottle of oil was.

Occasionally I was able to get it right, or at least narrow it down to 'groupings'. I might have been able to vaguely recognise a citrus scent but undetermined orange or lemon.

The small headway brought with it fleeting moments of happiness. It was such a genuine sense of victory when I was able to guess correctly. But the decline on my physical and mental health needed something greater than these fleeting moments, these baby steps. I desperately wanted my smell back, my life back.

However one of the offers of help after my media appearances came from Marc McDermott from NLP Training Ltd.

NLP (Neuro Linguistic Programming) wasn't something I knew much about. I approached with rational caution. A google search of the topic pulls up lots of information that suggests a type of Cognitive Behavioural Therapy (CBT), and hypnosis is also mentioned.

While supportive of CBT and its methods, hypnosis tends to conjure up a mental image of someone swinging a pendulum telling you that you're feeling sleepy, or making you behave like a chicken on a stage – so I had my reservations. I did not rush in with any expectations that this was the answer to all my problems, but equally I was ready to try anything. I was desperate to be cured.

By this point, I was nine months into doctors telling me there was nothing that could be done, that I might never recover, and I had made many unsuccessful other attempts to do so. I was prepared to do anything to get my life back, to smell and taste properly again. I agreed to an initial meet-up.

The initial consultation helped me understand what exactly was involved, and how it could help me. Despite the organisation name NLP training, Marc's approach is a combination of NLP, Time Line Therapy® and Hypnosis techniques.

It was interesting meeting because it encompassed a lot. There was just as much science as there was 'spiritual'. I felt reassured that it wasn't a gimmick, and while I could not say for certainty at this point if this was the solution, I left that first meeting feeling quite positive that it was something worth trying.

I had gone in weary and was quite open to him about that. But chatting about the process and the evidence behind it, logically it all seemed very sound and rational. I felt comfortable, he is obviously very intelligent and very knowledgeable in his field.

We discussed expectations and requirements for what I would need to be better and planned a date for our treatment session.

I do not claim to be an expert in NLP and the other techniques, far from it. There are much better information sources about it if you are interested in learning about it. There are practitioners across the world that will be able to tell you accurate and detailed information, and for anyone local or with the means to travel, I would of course encourage contacting Marc directly. To the best of my knowledge, he was the first person to cure this condition with his techniques. I searched every corner of the internet for a cure, and nothing came up before Marc found me.

If you want to be free of parosmia the greatest advice I can offer is to contact him. What I will tell you is an overview of the experience, to help explain in some way what the journey to overcome the condition was like, and to enhance your understanding of the steps involved.

The experience enabled me to understand better than ever the importance of language and its application. The things we set in motion simply by the things we think and say or allow ourselves to hear and take on board.

Doctors telling me - "You may never fully recover from this" – was the worst possible thing to say. Because internally it triggered something in me, that non-recovery was an option. Whereas I always needed to be certain I was going to get better.

The power we have is phenomenal. Every day we wake up, we breathe. We make cells. You cut yourself; your body stitches itself back up. It's not a conscious process, but something is pulling the strings, giving the instructions to do that. That's happening all the time, instructions, constantly.

We might not have conscious control over the 'background processes' running, but what we do have is conscious control about what instructions it might be registering. I was horrified to learn how many negative instructions I was giving off. Sometimes even by generic statements of one's health;

 "You're not going to get better / ever be back to normal" - being a critical one to parosmia recovery.

During the session, the glass kept breaking as I could link back so many of life's issues and problems to a source of my own creation. The way I was perceiving situations, the language I was using.

It became much bigger than curing my parosmia, it was the full picture. It was life-changing on a much wider scale. How I think about things, the terminology I use. The absolute power and control I have over my reality.

Over those two days, we explored so much more than just the issue of my smell. It was a full holistic analysis of what I was made up of, emotionally where everything, every emotion I felt and was capable of feeling originated. It was extraordinary.

It was discussion about my condition and so much more. It was visiting memories, so real it was like I was watching a movie of them. It was addressing language and the power of it. It was so much, and it was fascinating.

Again, I must reiterate I am in no way an expert and it reading this book is not the key to change your life, I just want it to give you the direction for where to go to get the help to do so.

Is there more to it than rejecting the statement that you won't recover? Of course, there is. My initial sessions were two, **full** days. Very intense days. I felt utterly consumed by the end of it.

It had been full of raw emotion. Concentration in ways I wasn't familiar with. Memory, honesty, connection, realisation. An experience like no other that is very hard to convey, I could not write it, I have struggled to even talk about it, to explain to friends and family exactly what took place over those two days.

I went home and all but collapsed in bed. Despite myself and wanting to know if it had worked, I was too tired to eat, too tired to shower, and as such, I didn't even register the significance of the change that had happened.

I slept through, undisturbed, but still awoke feeling tired. I got straight in the shower and let the water rouse me, rinse my face that still felt puffy from the previous few days.

Then, as I came to wash, I noticed was that my shower smelt like soap. Raspberries and lime to be exact, exactly like the bottle told me it should. Another inhale confirmed the sweetness of the raspberry against the tang of the lime. It had been so long since I had smelt sweetness, or tang.

I started to tear up as I turned to the shelving to pick up various bathroom products, gels and shampoos smelling them, registering the different fragrances, how they varied. Registering the absence of rot and foulness that had become so familiar.

The tears became sobs of joy. I documented the moment with a picture to share with people the news that it had worked. My eyes are tear soaked, hair wet from the shower, but you can tell I am elated.

I brushed my teeth and it tasted of mint. Cool, refreshing mint, my breath felt fresh. I burst out crying all over again.

Relief flooded me, hope flooded me. The weight of everything I had been carrying for eleven months, almost a full year of living this way, lifted.

That first week, so many people pointed out a difference in me. That my eyes seemed brighter; my smile wider, more genuine than it had in months. It turns out I had not been doing such a good job of concealing how badly affected I was to some.

That memory of that first weekend will stay with me forever. It fell at a time my friends' band were performing what was the first live music gig post-pandemic. Everyone in the audience was embracing a life they had missed that night. Laughing, dancing, clutching one another as they swayed and sang along. It felt like a scene from a movie.

I rejoiced with them at the normality, but for me it was exceptionally special. I could smell the beers that sloshed about, the perfume of the people who greeted me.

Even the mustiness of the pub, the sweat of the band in full swing. I could smell my husband, my friends. Not just their perfumes or clothes, but *them*. Having that connection back fully with people, suddenly being aware of the aroma of people that I had not even realised had been a scent I'd been missing.

The next day was again spent with those friends, a barbeque, a social event that I'd come to dread. But I vividly remember walking around the garden, putting my nose to all the plants and flowers taking in their sweetness. Sampling foods at a buffet and delighting when it tasted good, rushing back for more.

That night I stayed out until 6am, high in the company of people I felt fresh adoration for and high on the knowledge that my old life was in reach again. That my life would no longer be constantly plagued by putrid odour, and everything debilitating that came with it.

That weekend, how special it was, will stay with me forever. That weekend, I fell in love with life again.

At this point, I was not cured completely. I was able to smell many things correctly, although my sense of smell was much weaker. I had to intensely sniff things to get the impact. Food I saw a massive improvement with but some things still carried 'the taste.' Meat in the main was still difficult, green peppers. The things that had been the biggest offenders through the height of the condition lingered on.

But the difference it made so immediately was staggering. I was far less restricted in what I could eat. The smell that I was so used to incessantly invading my nostrils was no longer constant. I started to be able to experience smells again as I should.

At Marc's recommendation I tracked my macros too. It was eye-opening to see just how few calories I had been consuming, and how little nutritive value had been in the limited diet I had experienced for almost a year.

I was hardly getting any proteins or minerals from the food I had been able to eat. It became so obvious suddenly while I was constantly fatigued, breathless.

Falling apart. Tracking gave me insight into what I was lacking, and then I could take meaningful supplements to make up the deficit. I almost laughed that the whole time I'd been trialing weeds and oils and antler scrapings when all along iron and vitamins were part of the solution.

Physically the weight, *healthy* weight, started to creep back on. I just felt a renewed sense of energy with not just the hope, but the actual resounding confident knowledge that normality would come again for me.

My breathing became much less laboured. I was still unfit, two years exercise free will do that though. I was no longer restricted from doing basic things; carrying washing up the stairs or taking a walk of an evening.

One of perhaps the most unusual things was the requirement to re-learn some smells. Frequently, we would be out walking and I would get a whiff of something and have to clarify – what am I smelling? But not in the way I'd reluctantly become familiar with. With parosmia every smell was bad, so when I'd query smells, it was to understand what it was supposed to smell like. This was a pleasant or unique smell but as if my brain couldn't make the connection to what it belonged to. Like a baby fresh to the world I was experiencing and learning new aromas.

Over the following months, we had a few catch-up sessions which were more focussed on smells and tastes that I continued to struggle with. I wanted to get better immediately. I wanted to be as though none of this had ever happened. But repair takes time. We focused in our sessions on looking forward when it mattered most to be cured. If it couldn't be straight away, when did it have to be by, what was my "deadline"?

Immediately I thought of holidays. We love to travel and delight to sample the diversity many countries across the world have to offer. That feeling of experiencing a different culture is something I thrive from, and a huge part of that is the food. The idea of an all-inclusive holiday eating the same buffet food night after night just doesn't appeal. We go away and find restaurants off the beaten track and hunt out where the locals are eating. Try the cuisines no matter how unusual. As a rule of thumb with food I have a motto – "I'll try anything once." If I don't like it fine but, at least I've tried it.

After two years of not travelling, we had a big trip booked for March and April. Starting with a group holiday for a friend's wedding in Dubai, and then on to a more romantic couples' getaway to a luxury resort in Thailand.

Having been to Thailand before I know there are constant aromas there; a myriad of spices, street foods, massage oils, sand and sea, exotic plants; all assaulting your nose constantly. I could picture aspects of the holiday so clearly in my head it was more like viewing a memory, rather than something that was yet to happen. I could remember favourite dishes from previous visits. Favourite smells.

As much as I wanted my smell and taste fully back to normal right away, this was the true goal for me. Being on holiday somewhere where a working sense of smell was part of the experience. Embedding myself in the culture fully by trying and enjoying local foods and holiday smells.

Reconnecting with my husband somewhere we could both get the break we deserved after two difficult years.

Everything else faded for me, long-term plans on hold while I just put all my focus toward this holiday, and how I was going to experience it fully in every possible way.

The holiday was my target to be fully cured, and the focus of sessions was picturing everything so vividly that when I thought about it, it felt more like a memory then an event yet to occur.

Almost two years to the day the country went into lock down, and one year from me going to the doctors desperately seeking resolution for my declining health, we travelled to Dubai and then on to Thailand across March and April 2022. At last.

Chapter 5

Twelve Months On

Phuket province of Thailand boasts white sand beaches, turquoise oceans, and slightly inland thick, lush jungle. It is certainly a paradise location. Although it is hot, it is quite humid and prone to short but intense thunderstorms. Warm downpours.

On our first day of exploring the village, I remember thinking – I can smell rain. Thick in the air the smell hung, it was still dry but I could smell it, the moisture threatening. I was right, moments later we found ourselves soaked, and our clothes stuck to us as monsoon rain erupted from the skies.

With no point seeking shelter and already drenched through, we carried on walking amidst the rain, only stopping occasionally to wring my dress to keep it from weighing down my legs as I walked. But I didn't care, because I was happy, intensely happy. Not only was I no longer smelling putrid smells, but I was able to smell things normally again, even the rain in the sky. The smell of damp as material clings to skin.

On that holiday I exultantly dined on creamy Panang curries, rich satay, and spicy noodles. I sipped Mai Tai's, somehow sweet and tart at the same time. I smelt the salt that crisped up my hair after a swim in the sea. I kissed my husband and inhaled the scent of him and felt electricity. Having my senses back meant everything to me there.

My memories are laced with fragrances and aromas I revelled in. When I think about that holiday the memories carry every sense. It was more than just a trip for me it signified a significant milestone, a life experience. I can close my eyes and be transported back there simply recalling the smells, the tastes, everything that holiday became and represented for me.

Most of all that memory was a perfect match for the visual goal I had set, to be there, experiencing it all with no restrictions. I was cured.

The whole experience has left me with such a newfound appreciation for smell, and how important it is. It would be wrong for me to say "I live in fear of losing it again," – because living in fear is no way to live. I would not wish to endure anosmia or parosmia again but suspect it could be different for me with the mentality I've inherited from my experiences.

The mind-set of understanding how much control I have over what happens to me. My emotions and resilience to things. Twelve months ago, I was in a truly terrible place, worse than many perhaps realised. I'm not there now. Yes, because my smell and taste are back, my weight is back, my general health is back.

Additionally, my whole outlook is different now. The sessions I underwent unlocked something deeper in me than just getting my smell back. I've even noticed changes to what I can physically see and how my thought processes are. How I approach situations.

It's improved my ability to connect with people too, both in pre-existing relationships and new ones, which I hold such value in.

The appreciation for closeness with people was something I've always had but has only been enhanced by the pandemic, both the requirement to isolate away and my involuntary withdrawal from close social connection at the hands of parosmia. It's difficult to put into words how it's developed. But now I feel a pull, almost magnetic to certain people in my life, and have developed resilience to even things like sleep if it means spending more physical time in their presence. I feel such connection to them; I treasure every opportunity to be encompassed by the fragrance of them, to see and smell and taste the very colour of them.

Connection is everything. I am sure I am not alone in saying that not being able to connect was one of the most difficult parts of lock down. So having that back, supplementary to before, has been incredible. Yes it isn't for everyone and it is not for everyone, but if you find someone willing to let you really connect with them in such a way it is so special.

I feel a sense of importance and value for my own body and its functionality. My mind and subconscious, the things it is capable of. The power of the influence I have.

My entire goal when I set out on this journey was to get myself 'back to normal'. The reality has been quite different. Instead of reverting back to a state, I've come forward, I've changed. I have my smell and my taste as it once was. But I've inherited more along the way. I haven't gone back to a version of myself that once existed but instead grown into something better.

So once again, I will say, I am not an expert in NLP, or any of the other techniques I underwent. But I am a champion of it. I went in sceptical, but I saw massive results, far exceeding the purpose and expectations of why I went in the first place. As a champion now, I want to get several messages out there.

Firstly, to people suffering parosmia, I'm sorry. I know and understand what you are going through. The burden of it. But, you will recover. Please know that you absolutely can and will.

To others, please consider the impact of language. How easy is it to unconsciously embed something in someone, how damaging! Especially if you are in a position of trust or recognised as an expert or authority. Someone in the medical profession please never say "You won't get better." Please don't even say "You might not." Shifting your language and your focus will have such a massive impact and I embolden you to explore this.

Consider the impact of language on yourself too. If you stop and think about it, you will realise how many of the restrictions and rules that bind you are self-inflicted.

You might find that it changes your life.

Thank you

Thank you to anyone taking the time to read this. I've written before, but never so personally. Exposing yourself in such a way leaves you feeling vulnerable, but I hope it is for good reason and purpose.

Thank you to my husband, friends and family, for getting me through it as far as you did. I love you all deeply.

Thank you to Marc McDermott – for reaching out, for all your help and time. For the journey.

Thank you to Liz, for being my editor, especially the little smatterings of love between genuine feedback which made me smile.

ABOUT THE AUTHOR

Sally McCreith

Sally works full time running a healthcare education service, but has always been a keen writer. Her works are normally that of fiction, but following her experience with long covid and parosmia took pen to paper to share her experience.

Outside of work, Sally lives for enjoying good food and drink, live music, taking pictures of sunsets and silly faces; and spending time in the company of the people she loves.

RESOURCES

NLP Sessions

A massive thank you too to Marc, for reaching out, and showing me how to overcome. He can be contacted via;

https://www.nlptraining.org.uk/

info@nlptraining.org.uk

Abscent

This charity is dedicated to people with loss of smell and work hard to offer support. I found helpful coping mechanisms here as well as able to network with people going through the same experience, which was invaluable to my mental health

https://abscent.org/

Printed in Great Britain
by Amazon